CONTENTS

Bees aren't worried about a cactus's sharp spines.

Bees and Flowers

By Kevin Cunningham

21st Century Junior Library

Published in the United States of America by
Cherry Lake Publishing
Ann Arbor, Michigan
www.cherrylakepublishing.com

Content Adviser: Stephen Ditchkoff, Professor of Wildlife Ecology and Management, Auburn University, Alabama
Reading Adviser: Marla Conn MS, Ed., Literacy specialist, Read-Ability, Inc.

Photo Credits: © Jeff Zehnder/Shutterstock, cover, 1, 12; © arka38/Shutterstock, 4; © Marie C Fields/Shutterstock, 6; © Edouard Coleman/Shutterstock, 8; © Zeljko Radojko/Shutterstock, 10; © ducu59us/Shutterstock, 14; © ValentynVolkov/istock, 16; © Fotochip/Shutterstock, 18; © Serg64/Shutterstock, 20

Library of Congress Cataloging-in-Publication Data

CIP data has been filed and is available at catalog.loc.gov

Cherry Lake Publishing would like to acknowledge the work of The Partnership for 21st Century Skills. Please visit *www.p21.org* for more information.

Printed in the United States of America
Corporate Graphics

Partners

Did you know the fruits and vegetables we eat depend on bees? The same is true for **cacti**. Without bees, we would have few flowers for Mother's Day. Trees would find it hard to grow, too.

Bees and plants share an important **relationship**. Their teamwork makes human and animal life possible. Bees may be small. But they have a huge effect on our world.

This tulip has bright yellow pollen. Its pollen helps ensure that there will be new tulip plants.

Amazing Pollen

Bees eat the **pollen** inside flowers. Pollen keeps bees healthy and gives them energy. Bees work all the time. They need as much energy as they can get.

Pollen looks like dust. Many plants have yellow pollen. Other plant pollen may be a different color. Most plants make pollen shaped like a spiky ball.

Each tiny apple seed can become a new apple tree and each apple tree can produce many new apples.

Plants use pollen to **reproduce**. All living things must reproduce. Birds lay eggs. Humans have babies. And most plants make seeds.

Plants reproduce in many different ways. Pine trees use cones. Moss can send out shoots to start a new “baby” plant.

Look!

Look inside an apple or cucumber. What do you find? Seeds, of course. The parts of fruits and vegetables we eat surround seeds. They protect the seeds. They help seeds grow into new plants.

There are many different kinds of flowers,
but all flowers need help from bees and other insects.

Flowering plants reproduce with seeds. To make seeds, pollen must move from one flower to another. Bees are one creature that make that happen.

Bees carry pollen on their legs. One bee can carry almost half its body weight in pollen.

Inside the Flower

Pollen covers a part of the flower called the **anther**. The anther sits at the end of a stalk inside a flower.

Bees land on the anther to eat. Dusty pollen gets all over the bee. The bee flies off. It visits another flower. The pollen it carries rubs off onto that flower's **stigma**. A stigma grows in the middle of a flower. It is sticky.

PARTS OF A FLOWER

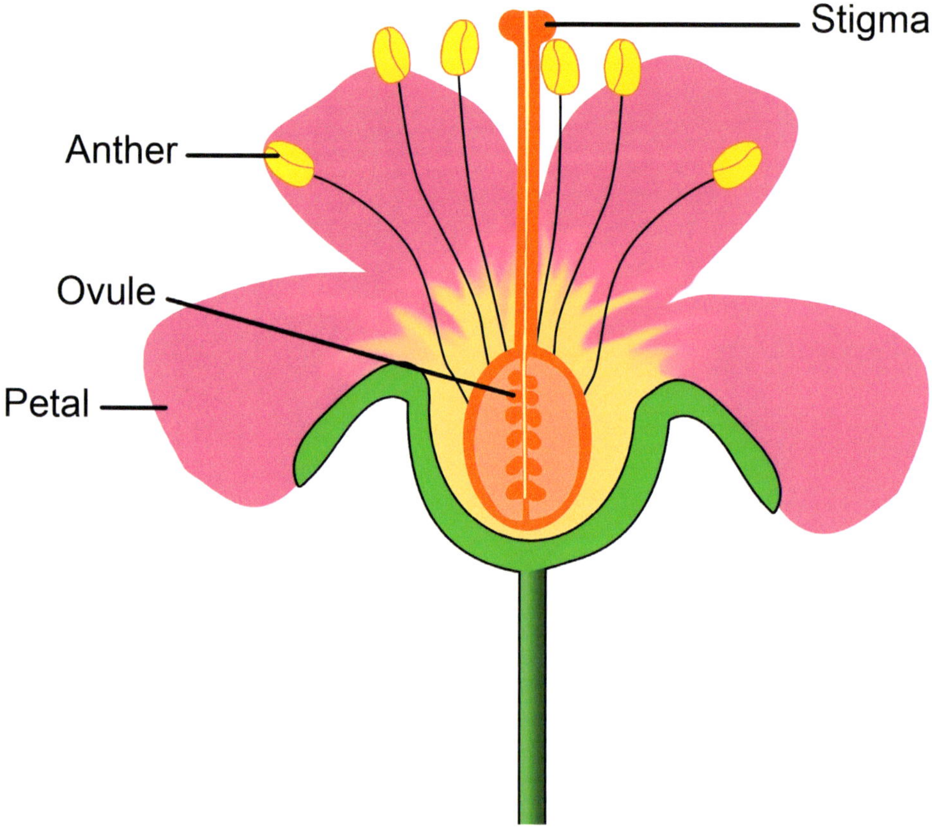

Flowers have to look attractive to bees.

A tube grows from a flake of pollen into the stigma. The pollen follows the tube. Inside, it combines with a part of the plant called an **ovule**. Together, the pollen and ovule grow into a seed. The seed becomes a new plant, fruit, or vegetable.

Scientists call this process **pollination**. The plant needs pollination to reproduce.

Ask Questions!

Sunflowers and pumpkins give humans two popular seed snacks. Find out what other plants grow seeds we need. Look up wheat and corn online or in a book. What foods do we make from their seeds?

Honey bees must visit about two million flowers to make 1 pound (.45 kilograms) of honey.

Sweet Work

Plants also make **nectar**. One kind of bee, the honey bee, uses nectar to make **honey**. Honey bees eat honey. So do we!

Nectar forms inside a flower. The honey bee's straw-like tongue sucks it in. The bee keeps the sweet nectar in its **honey stomach**. The honey stomach has nothing to do with eating. Bees use it only for storing liquid. A honey stomach full of

Some people raise bees and harvest their honey.
These people are called beekeepers.

nectar weighs about as much as the honey bee itself.

A honey bee lives in a hive. Hundreds or thousands of bees share a hive. At the hive, the honey bee passes the nectar to **house bees**. The house bees chew up the nectar. Chewing gets rid of extra water.

Soon the house bees cough up a thick syrup. They push the syrup into small pockets in the hive. The dried syrup becomes honey. Honey bees cover the pockets of new honey with wax. The honey stays there until the bees need to eat it.

Without bees and other insects, we would have no flowers or fruits.

Bees help flowering plants reproduce. Flowers give honey bees important food. Each helps the other. It is one of nature's most amazing relationships.

Create!

It is easy to make honey biscuits or scones. You will mix honey with flour, butter, baking powder, milk, and an egg. Find a recipe in a book or online. Ask an adult to help.

GLOSSARY

anther (AN-thur) the part of the plant with pollen

cacti (KAK-tye) spiny plants that live in the desert

flowering plants (FLOU-ur-ing PLANTS) plants that grow flowers

honey (HUN-ee) a sweet, sticky food made by bees

honey stomach (HUN-ee STUM-ek) a second stomach bees use to carry nectar

house bees (HOUS BEEZ) bees that chew nectar to form honey

nectar (NEK-tur) a sweet liquid found inside of flowers

ovule (OV-yool) a plant part that becomes a seed after pollination

pollen (PAH-luhn) dusty grains that grow in flowers

pollination (pah-luh-NAY-shun) moving pollen from the anther to the stigma

relationship (ri-LAY-shuhn-ship) a connection

reproduce (ree-pruh-DOOS) to create new versions of a living thing

stigma (STIG-muh) the part of a flower that receives pollen

FIND OUT MORE

BOOKS

Huber, Raymond, with Brian Lovelock. *Flight of the Honey Bee*. Somerville, MA: Candlewick, 2013.

Slade, Suzanne, with Carol Schwartz. *What If There Were No Bees?* North Mankato, MN: Picture Window Books, 2011.

Spilsbury, Louise. *How Bees Make Honey*. North Mankato, MN: Capstone, 2010.

WEB SITES

DK Find Out!—Parts of a Flower
www.dkfindout.com/us/animals-and-nature/plants/parts-flower

Yakima Valley Museum—Pollination
http://yakimavalleymuseum.org/apple/journey03.cfm

INDEX

ABOUT THE AUTHOR

Kevin Cunningham is the author of more than 60 books for children. He lives near Chicago.